THE AMAZING SECRET OF
THE SOULS IN PURGATORY

THE AMAZING SECRET OF
THE SOULS IN PURGATORY

by Sister Emmanuel of Medjugorje

Queenship

PUBLISHING COMPANY

P.O Box 42028 Santa Barbara, CA 93140-2028

(800) 647-9882 • (805) 957-4893 • Fax: (805) 957-1631

Library of Congress #: 97-67584

Published by:
Queenship Publishing
P.O. Box 42028
Santa Barbara, CA 93140-2028
(800) 647-9882 • (805) 957-4893 • Fax: (805) 957-1631

Printed in the United States of America

ISBN: 1-57918-004-3

Contents

1 - This Booklet Fills a Void 1

2 - The Interview with Maria Simma 7

3 - A Proposition to All 45

4 - Don't Forget About Indulgences! 51

Fr. Angelico - *Discesa al Limbo*
(The Descent into Limbo)

This Booklet Fills a Void

O ne day, I read with great interest a book about the souls in Purgatory. It struck me so much because it related very recent testimonies and also explained very well the Church's doctrine on the subject. It is a book by Maria Simma, called *The Souls in Purgatory Told Me...* Straight away, I wrote to the editor who told me that Maria Simma is still alive. Quickly, I contacted her and she agreed to meet me to answer my questions, which were many!

I was delighted, because each time I have the opportunity to speak or preach on the poor souls, I've found that there is an immense, extraordinary interest on the part of my listeners. Often, they beg me to tell them more, pushing me further, asking me: "Tell us more, other things about these souls." I saw clearly that this fulfilled a vital thirst, a thirst to know what is waiting for us, each of us, after death.

It must be said too that these things are scarcely taught any more in parishes, in regular catechism, in chaplaincies, practically nowhere. So there's a great emptiness, a great lack, if you prefer, a great ignorance, even a certain anguish in the face of these realities of the final things.

Therefore, this booklet will help us not only to get rid of this anguish once and for all, with regard to Purgatory but will also enlighten us, hopefully, and enable us to understand that God's plan for us, for our destiny, is absolutely magnificent, splendid, worthy of our enthusiasm! Also, that we have in our hands an immense power on this earth to give happiness to the souls of our departed, for one thing, and to find that happiness for ourselves as well, in our own lives.

Today, Maria Simma is 82; she lives alone in her little house in Sonntag, a very lovely village in the Vorarlberg mountains in Austria, and that is where I met her.

Who is Maria Simma?

A simple country woman who, since her childhood, has prayed a great deal for the souls in Purgatory. When she was twenty-five, she was favored with a very particular charism in the Church, very rare too, the charism of being visited by the souls in Purgatory. She is a fervent Catholic and has a great humility — this struck me a lot; she has a great simplicity too. She is very much encouraged in her task by her parish priest and her bishop. In spite of the quite extraordinary character of her charism, she lives in real poverty. For example, in her little room we hardly had enough space to move around the chairs she had offered us...

An extraordinary charism? Yes, but which obviously has deep roots in the history of the Church, for many are the saints — canonized or not — who have exercised this charism. I could mention, for example, St. Gertrude, St. Catherine of Genoa, who wrote much on the subject, Maryam of Jesus, St. Margaret Mary of Paray-le-Monial who had the vision of the Sacred Heart, the Holy Curé of Ars, Blessed Faustina, St. John Bosco, Blessed Maryam of Bethlehem, etc. A book could be written on the subject; in fact I think several have! When we look closely at the teachings of these saints, we see that all of them say the same thing; and Maria Simma for her part only relives their beautiful testimony.

This is why I did not hesitate to interview her, as she has the advantage for us of living in our times, and is willing to make herself available. You can easily imagine that I swamped her with questions, I made the most of it!... The problem is she doesn't speak a word of French, and for this reason I had to use an interpreter.

For the sake of brevity and clarity I will sum up some of Maria's answers and, at other times, give you the translation of her own words. I will also add, here and there, my personal comments.

Domenico Beccafumi - *Cristo al Limbo*
(Christ's Descent into Limbo)

The Interview
with Maria Simma

The First Time

Maria, can you tell us how you were visited for the first time by a soul in Purgatory?

Yes, it was in 1940. One night, around 3 or 4 o'clock in the morning, I heard someone coming into my bedroom. This woke me up; I looked to see who on earth could have walked into my bedroom.

Where you afraid?

No, I'm not at all fearful. Even when I was a little child, my mother said I was a special child because I was never afraid.

So, that night... tell us!

Well, I saw a complete stranger. He walked back and forth slowly. I said to him severely: "How did you get in here? Go away!" But he continued to walk impatiently around the bedroom, as if he hadn't heard. So I asked him

*again: "What are you doing?" But as he still didn't an-
swer, I jumped out of bed and tried to grab him, but I
grasped only air. There was nothing there. So I went back
to bed, but again I heard him pacing back and forth.*

*I wondered how I could see this man, but I couldn't
grab him. I rose again to hold onto him and stop him walk-
ing around; again, I grasped only emptiness.*

*Puzzled, I went back to bed. He didn't come back, but
I couldn't get back to sleep. The next day, after Mass, I
went to see my spiritual director and told him everything.
He told me that if this should happen again, I shouldn't
ask, "Who are you?" but " What do you want from me?"*

*The following night, the man returned, definitely the
same man. I asked him "What do you want from me?" He
replied: "Have three Masses celebrated from me and I will
be delivered."*

*So I understood that it was a soul in Purgatory. My
spiritual father confirmed this.*

*He also advised me never to turn away the poor souls,
but to accept with generosity whatever they asked of me.*

And afterwards, the visits continued?

*Yes. For several years, there were only three or four
souls, above all in November. Afterwards, there were more.*

A Love-Wound

What do these souls ask of you?

*In most cases, they ask to have Masses celebrated
and that one be present at these Masses; they ask to have*

the rosary said and also that one make the Stations of the Cross.

At this point, the major question is raised: What exactly is Purgatory? I'd say that it's a marvelous invention of God. Let me give you an image which is my own. Suppose that one day a door opens, and a splendid being appears, extremely beautiful, of a beauty that has never been seen on earth. You are fascinated, overwhelmed by this being of light and beauty, even more so that this being shows that he is madly in love with you — you have never dreamed of being loved so much. You sense too that he has a great desire to draw you to him, to be one with you. And the fire of love which burns in your heart impels you to throw yourself into his arms.

But wait — you realize at this moment that you haven't washed for months and months, that you smell bad; your nose is runing, your hair is greasy and matted, there are big dirty stains on your clothes, etc. So you say to yourself, "No, I just can't present myself in this state. First I must go and wash: a good shower, then straight away I'll come back."

But the love which has been born in your heart is so intense, so burning, so strong, that this delay for the shower is absolutely unbearable. And the pain of the absence, even if it only lasts for a couple of minutes, is an atrocious wound in the heart, proportional to the intensity of the revelation of the love — it is a "love-wound."

Purgatory is exactly this. It's a delay imposed by our impurity, a delay before God's embrace, a wound of love which causes intense suffering, a waiting, if you like, a nostalgia for love. It is precisely this burning, this longing which cleanses us of whatever is still impure in us. Purgatory is a place of desire, a mad desire for God, desire for this God whom we already know, for we have seen him, but with whom we are not yet united.

Now I am going to ask Maria to clarify a fundamental point:

Maria, do the souls in Purgatory have, nevertheless, joy and hope in the midst of their suffering?

Yes. No soul would want to come back from Purgatory to the earth. They have knowledge which is infinitely beyond ours. They just could not decide to return to the darkness of the earth.

Here we see the difference from the suffering that we know on earth. In Purgatory, even if the pain of the soul is terrible, there is the certitude of living forever with God. It's an unshakable certitude. The joy is greater than the pain. There is nothing on earth which could make them want to live here again, where one is never sure of anything.

Maria, can you tell us now if it is God who sends a soul into Purgatory, or if the soul itself decides to go there?

It is the soul itself which wants to go to Purgatory, in order to be pure before going to Heaven.

The souls in Purgatory adhere fully to God's will; they rejoice in the good, they desire our good and they love very much: they love God, and they love us too. They are perfectly united to the Spirit of God, the light of God.

Maria, at the moment of death, does one see God in full light or in an obscure manner?
In a manner still obscure, but, all the same, in such brightness that this is enough to cause great longing.

Actually, it's such a dazzling brightness compared with the darkness of the earth! And it's still nothing compared with the full light the soul will know when it arrives in Heaven. Here we can refer to "near death experiences." The soul is so drawn by this light that it is agony for it to return to earth in its body, after this experience.

Charity Covers a Multitude of Sins

Maria, can you tell us what the role of Our Lady is with the souls in Purgatory?
She comes often to console them and to tell them they have done many good things. She encourages them.

Are there any days in particular on which she delivers them?
Above all, Christmas Day, All Saints Day, Good Friday, the Feast of the Assumption, and the Ascension of Jesus.

Maria, why does one go to Purgatory? What are the sins which most lead to Purgatory?

Sins against charity, against the love of one's neighbor, hardness of heart, hostility, slandering, calumny — all these things.

Saying wicked things and calumny are among the worst blemishes which require a long purification.

Yes.

Here, Maria gives us an example which really struck her which I would like to share with you.

She had been asked to find out if a woman and a man were in Purgatory.

To the great astonishment of those who had asked, the woman was already in Heaven and the man was in Purgatory. In fact, this woman had died while undergoing an abortion, whereas the man often went to church and apparently led a worthy, devout life.

So Maria searched for more information, thinking she'd been mistaken — but no, it was true. They had died at practically the same moment, but the woman had experienced deep repentance, and was very humble, whereas the man criticized everyone; he was always complaining and saying bad things about others. This is why his Purgatory lasted so long. And Maria concluded: *"We mustn't judge on appearances."*

Other sins against charity are all our rejections of certain people we do not like, our refusals to make peace, our refusals to forgive, and all the bitterness we store inside.

Maria also illustrated this point with another example which gave us food for thought. It's the story of a woman she knew very well. This lady died and was in Purgatory, in the most terrible Purgatory, with the most atrocious sufferings. And when she came to see Maria, she explained why: she had had a female friend; between them arose a great enmity, caused by herself. She had maintained this enmity for years and years, even though her friend had many times asked for peace, for reconciliation. But each time she refused. When she fell gravely ill, she continued to close her heart, to refuse the reconciliation offered by her friend, right up to her deathbed. I believe that this example has great significance concerning rancor which is maintained. And our words, too, can be destructive: we can never emphasize enough how much a critical or bitter word can truly kill — but also, on the contrary, how much a word can heal.

Maria, please tell us: who are those who have the greatest chance of going straight to Heaven?

Those who have a good heart towards everyone. Love covers a multitude of sins.

Yes, Saint Paul himself tells us this!

What are the means which we can take on earth to avoid Purgatory and go straight to Heaven?

We must do a great deal for the souls in Purgatory, for they help us in their turn. We must have much humility; this is the greatest weapon against evil, against the Evil One. Humility drives evil away.

I can't resist telling you a very lovely testimony of Father Berlioux (who wrote a wonderful book on the souls in Purgatory), concerning the help offered by these souls to those who relieve them by their prayer and sufferages.

He tells the story of a person particularly devoted to the poor souls who had consecrated her life to their relief.

"At the hour of her death, she was attacked with fury by the demon who saw her at the point of escaping from him. It seemed that the entire abyss was united against her, surrounding her with its infernal troops.

"The dying woman struggled excruciatingly for some time when suddenly she saw entering her apartment, a crowd of unknown people of dazzling beauty, who put the demon to flight and, approaching her bed, spoke to her with the most heavenly encouragement and consolations. With her last breath, in great joy, she cried: 'Who are you? Who are you, please, you who do so much good to me?'

"The benevolent visitors replied: 'We are inhabitants of Heaven, whom your help has led to Beatitude. And we in our turn come in gratitude to help you cross the threshold of eternity and rescue you from this place of anguish to bring you into the joy of the Holy City.'

"At these words, a smile lit up the face of the dying woman, her eyes closed and she fell asleep in the peace of the Lord. Her soul, pure as a dove, presented to the Lord of lords, found as many protectors and advocates as souls she had delivered, and recognized worthy of glory, she entered in triumph, among the applause and blessings of all those she had rescued from Purgatory. May we, one day, have the same happiness."

The souls delivered by our prayer are extremely grateful: they help us in our lives; it's most perceptible. I strongly recommend that you experience this yourself! They do help us; they know our needs and obtain many graces for us.

Maria, I am thinking of the Good Thief who was next to Jesus on the Cross. I really would like to know what he did for Jesus to promise him that this very day onwards, he would be in the Kingdom with him?

He humbly accepted his suffering, saying that it was justice. And he encouraged the other thief to accept his too. He had the fear of God, which means humility.

Another beautiful example related by Maria Simma shows how a good action makes up for a whole life of sin. Let's hear it from Maria herself:

"I knew a young man of about twenty, in a nearby village. This young man's village had been cruelly stricken by a series of avalanches which had killed a large number of people.

"One night, this young man was in his parents' house when he heard an avalanche just next door to his house. He heard piercing screams, heartrending screams, 'Save us! Come, save us! We are trapped beneath the avalanche!'

"Leaping up, he rose from his bed and rushed downstairs to go to the rescue of these people. His mother had heard the screams and prevented him from leaving; she blocked the door, saying 'No! Let others go and help them, not always us! It's too dangerous outside, I don't want yet another death!' But he, because he had been deeply affected by these screams, really wanted to go to the rescue of these people; he pushed his mother aside. He said to her: *'Yes! I'm going! I can't let them die like this!'* He went out, and then he himself, on the path, was struck by an avalanche and was killed.

"Three days after his death, he comes to visit me, at night, and he says to me: *'Have three Masses said for me; by this, I will be delivered from Purgatory.'* I went to inform his family and friends; they were astonished to know that after only three Masses, he would be delivered from Purgatory. His friends said to me: 'Oh, I wouldn't have liked to have been in his place in the moment of death, if you'd seen all the bad things he'd done!'

"But this young man said to me: *'You see, I'd made an act of pure love in risking my life for these people; it's thanks to this that the Lord welcomed me so quickly into his Heaven. Yes, charity covers a multitude of sins...'*"

This story shows us that charity, a single act of love given freely, had been sufficient to purify this young man from a dissolute life; and the Lord had made the most of this moment of love. Maria in fact added that this young man might never again have had the opportunity to offer such a great act of love, and might have turned bad. The Lord, in his mercy, took him just at the moment when he appeared before him at his most beautiful, most pure, because of this act of love.

It is very important, at the hour of death, to abandon oneself to God's will.

Maria told me of the case of a mother of four children who was about to die. Instead of rebelling and worrying, she said to the Lord: "I accept death, as long as it is your will, and I put my life in your hands. I entrust my sons to you and I know that you will take care of them."

Maria said that, because of her immense trust in God, this woman went straight to Heaven and avoided Purgatory.

Therefore, we really can say that love, humility and abandonment to God are the three golden keys to going directly to Heaven.

Offer a Mass for Them

Maria, can you now tell us what are the most effective means to help deliver the souls in Purgatory?
  The most efficient means is the Mass.

Why the Mass?
  Because it is Christ who offers himself out of love for us. It is the offering of Christ himself to God, the most

beautiful offering. The priest is God's representative, but it is God himself who offers himself and sacrifices himself for us. The efficacy of the Mass for the deceased is even greater for those who attached great value to the Mass during their lives. If they attended Mass and prayed with all their hearts, if they went to Mass on weekdays — according to their time available — they draw great profit from Masses celebrated for them. Here, too, one harvests what one has sown.

A soul in Purgatory sees very clearly on the day of his funeral if we really pray for him or if we have simply made an act of presence to show we were there. The poor souls say that tears are no good to them, only prayer. Often they complain that people go to a funeral without addressing a single prayer to God, while shedding many tears; this is useless!

Concerning the Mass, I will quote a beautiful example given by the Curé of Ars to his parishioners. He told them:

"My children, a good priest had the unhappiness to lose a friend he cherished tenderly, and so he prayed very much for the repose of his soul.

"One day, God made known to him that his friend was in Purgatory and suffered terribly. The holy priest believed that he could do no better than to offer the Holy Sacrifice of the Mass for his dear friend who had died. At the moment of the consecration, he took the host between his fin-

gers and said 'Holy Eternal Father, let us make an exchange. You hold the soul of my friend who is in Purgatory, and I hold the Body of Your Son in my hands. Well, good and merciful Father, deliver my friend and I offer you your Son with all the merits of his death and Passion.'

"The request was answered. In fact, at the moment of the elevation, he saw the soul of his friend, shining in glory, rising to Heaven; God had accepted the deal.

"My children, when we want to deliver from Purgatory a soul dear to us, let us do the same: let us offer to God, through the Holy Sacrifice, his Beloved Son with all the merits of his death and Passion. He will not be able to refuse us anything."

Don't Waste Your Earthly Sufferings

There is another means, very powerful, to help the poor souls: the offering of our sufferings, our penance, such as fasting, renunciations, etc. — and of course involuntary suffering like illness or mourning.

Maria, you have been invited many times to suffer for the poor souls, in order to deliver them. Can you tell us what you have experienced and undergone during these times?

The first time, a soul asked me if I wouldn't mind suffering for three hours in my body, for her, and that afterwards I could resume working. I said to myself: "If it will all be over after three hours, I could accept it." During these three hours, I had the impression that they lasted three days, it was so painful. But at the end, I looked at my watch, and I saw that it had only lasted three hours. The soul told me that by accepting that suffering with love for three hours, I had saved her twenty years of Purgatory!

Yes, but why did you suffer for only three hours to avoid twenty years of Purgatory? What did your sufferings have that was worth more?

It is because suffering on earth does not have the same value. On earth, when we suffer, we can grow in love, we can gain merits, which is not the case with the sufferings in Purgatory. In Purgatory, the sufferings serve only to purify us from sin. On earth, we have all the graces. We have the freedom to choose.

All this is so encouraging because it gives an extraordinary meaning to our sufferings; the suffering which is offered, voluntary or involuntary, even the smallest sacrifices we can make, suffering or sickness, mourning, disappointment... if we live them with patience, if we welcome them in humility, these sufferings can have an unheard-of power to help souls.

The best thing to do, Maria tells us, is to unite our sufferings to those of Jesus, by placing them in the hands of Mary. She is the one who knows best how to use them, since often we ourselves do not know the most urgent needs around us.

All this, of course, Mary will give back to us at the hour of our death.

You see, these sufferings offered will be our most precious treasures in the other world. We must remind each other of this and encourage each other when we suffer.

And Don't Begrudge Your Prayers

Another very effective means, Maria tells us, is the **Stations of the Cross**, because, by contemplating the sufferings of the Lord, we begin little by little to hate sin, and to desire salvation for all people. And this inclination of the heart brings great relief to the souls in Purgatory.

The Stations of the Cross also move us to repentance; we start repenting when faced with sin.

Another point, very helpful to the souls in Purgatory, is to say the **rosary**, all fifteen mysteries, for the sake of the deceased. Through the rosary, many souls are delivered from Purgatory each year; it must be said here as well that it is the Mother of God herself who comes to Purgatory to deliver the souls. This is very beautiful, because the souls in Purgatory call Our Lady the "Mother of Mercy."

The souls also tell Maria that **indulgences** have an inestimable value for their deliverance. It is sometimes cruel not to make use of this treasure that the Church proposes for the profit of souls. The subject of indulgences would be too long to explain here, but I can refer you to the marvelous text written by Paul VI in 1968 on the subject. You can ask your parish priest for it, or simply ask at your usual religious bookstore. (See Page 51)

Therefore, we can say that the great means of helping the souls in Purgatory is **prayer in general**; all kinds of prayer. Here I would like to give you the testimony of Hermann Cohen, a Jewish artist who converted to Catholicism in 1864 and greatly venerated the Eucharist. He left the world and entered a very austere religious order; he frequently adored the Blessed Sacrament for which he had a great veneration. During his adoration, he would beg the Lord to convert his mother, whom he loved so much. Well, his mother died without having been converted. So Hermann, sick with sorrow, prostrated himself before the Blessed Sacrament, in deep grief, praying: "Lord, I owe you everything, it is true. But what have I refused you? My youth, my hopes in the world, my well-being, the joys of a family, a rest — maybe well deserved — all sacrificed as soon as you called me. And you, Lord, Eternal Goodness, who promised to give back a hundredfold, you have refused me the soul of my mother. My God, I succumb to this martyrdom, I will stop my complaints." He cried his poor heart out. Suddenly, a mysterious voice struck his ear:

"Man of little faith! Your mother is saved. Know that prayer is all-powerful in my presence. I gathered all those you had addressed to me for your mother, and my Providence took account of her in her last hour.

"At the moment she expired, I came to her; she saw me and cried: 'My Lord and my God!' Have courage, your mother has avoided damnation and fervent supplication will soon deliver her soul from the bonds of Purgatory."

And we know that Father Hermann Cohen, soon afterwards, learned through a second apparition that his mother had risen to Heaven.

I recommend strongly as well the prayers of St. Bridget which are most recommended for the poor souls.

Let me add something important: the souls in Purgatory can no longer do anything for themselves; they are totally helpless. If the living do not pray for them, they are totally abandoned. Therefore, it is very important to realize the immense power, the incredible power that each one of us has in his hands to relieve these souls who suffer.

We wouldn't think twice about helping a child who has fallen in front of us from a tree and who had broken his bones. Of course, we would do everything for him! So, in the same way, we should take great care of these souls, who expect everything from us, attentive to the slightest offering, hopeful for the least of our prayers, to relieve them from their pain. And it might be the finest way to practice charity.

I think, for example, of the kindness of the Good Samaritan in the Gospel, towards the man left half-dead on the roadside bleeding from his wounds. This man depended completely on the good heart of the passerby.

Maria, why can one no longer gain merits in Purgatory, when one can on earth?

Because at the moment of death, the time to earn merits is over. For as long as we are living on earth, we can repair the evil we have done. The souls in Purgatory envy us this opportunity. Even the angels are jealous of us, for we have the possibility of growing for as long as we are on earth.

But often, the suffering in our lives leads us to rebellion and we have great difficulty in accepting and living it. How can we live suffering so that it bears fruit?

Sufferings are the greatest proof of the love of God, and if we offer them well they can win many souls.

But how can we welcome suffering as a gift and not as a punishment (as we often do), as a chastisement?

We must give everything to Our Lady. She is the one who knows best who needs such and such an offering in order to be saved.

On the subject of suffering, I would like to relate an extraordinary testimony that Maria told us of. It was in 1954, and a series of deadly avalanches had struck a village next to Maria's. Later, other avalanches had struck, but they had been stopped, in a completely miraculous way, before reaching the village, so that there was no damage.

The souls explained that in this village had died a woman who had been ill and was not properly treated; she had suffered terribly for thirty years. And she had offered all her sufferings for the sake of her village.

The souls explained to Maria that it was thanks to the offering of this woman that the village had been spared the avalanches.

She had borne her sufferings with patience. Maria tells us that if she had enjoyed good health, the village could not have been saved. She adds that sufferings borne with patience can save more souls than prayer (but prayer helps us to bear our sufferings).

We should not always consider suffering as a punishment. It can be accepted as expiation not only for ourselves but above all for others. Christ was innocence itself and he suffered the most for the expiation of our sins.

Only in Heaven will we know all that we have obtained by suffering with patience in union with the sufferings of Christ.

Maria, do the souls in Purgatory rebel when faced with their suffering?

No! They want to purify themselves; they understand that it is necessary.

At the Point of Death

What is the role of contrition or repentance at the moment of death?

Contrition is very important. The sins are forgiven, in any case, but there remain the consequences of sins. If one wishes to receive a full indulgence at the moment of death — that means going straight to Heaven — the soul has to be free from all attachment.

Here, I would like to share a very significant testimony given by Maria. She was asked to find out about a woman that her relations believed to be lost, because she had led an awful life. Well, she had an accident, she fell from a train and this accident killed her. A soul told Maria that this woman had been saved, saved from Hell, because at the moment of death, she said to God: "You are right to take my life, because in this way I will no longer be able to offend you." And this had erased all her sins. This example is highly significant, for it shows that a single moment of humility, of repentance at the moment of death, can save us. This doesn't mean that she did not go to Purgatory, but she avoided Hell which she perhaps deserved through her impiety.

Maria, I would like to ask you: at the moment of death, is there a time in which the soul still has the chance to turn towards God, even after a sinful life, before entering into eternity — a time, if you like, between apparent death and real death?

Yes, yes, the Lord gives several minutes to each one, in order to regret his sins and to decide: I accept or I do not accept to go see God. There, we see a film of our lives.

I knew a man who believed in the Church's teachings, but not in eternal life. One day, he fell gravely ill, and slid into a coma. He saw himself in a room with a board on which all his deeds were written, the good and the bad. Then the board disappeared as well as the walls of the room, and it was infinitely beautiful. Then he woke up from his coma and decided to change his life.

This is very much like the testimonies of "near death experiences"; the experience of the supernatural light is such that people can no longer live afterwards as they had lived before.

Maria, at the moment of death, does God reveal himself with the same intensity to all souls?

Each one is given knowledge of his life and also the sufferings to come; but it is not the same for everyone. The intensity of the Lord's revelation depends on each one's life.

Maria, does the devil have permission to attack us at the moment of death?

Yes, but man also has the grace to resist him, to push him away. So, if man does not want anything to do with him, the devil can do nothing.

That's good news! When someone knows he is going to die soon, what is for him the best way to get prepared?

To abandon himself totally to the Lord. Offer all his sufferings. Be completely happy in God.

And what attitude should one have before someone who is going to die? What is the best that one can do for him?

Pray hard! Prepare him for death; one must speak the truth.

Maria, what advice would you give to anyone who wants to become a saint here on earth?

Be very humble. We must not be occupied with ourselves. Pride is evil's greatest trap.

Maria, please tell us: can one ask the Lord to do one's Purgatory on earth, in order not to have to do it after death?

Yes. I knew a priest and a young woman who were both ill with tuberculosis in the hospital. The young woman said to the priest: "Let's ask the Lord to be able to suffer on earth as much as necessary in order to go straight to Heaven."

The priest replied that he himself didn't dare to ask for this. Nearby was a religious Sister who had overheard the whole conversation. The young woman died first, the priest died later, and he appeared to the Sister, saying: "If only I had had the same trust as this young woman, I too would have gone straight to Heaven."

Thank you, Maria, for this lovely testimony.

At this point, Maria asked for a five-minute break, as she had to go and feed her chickens... But the minute she returned, we continued with our questions.

The "Occupants" of Purgatory

Maria, are there different degrees in Purgatory?

Yes, there is a great difference of degree of moral suffering. Each soul has a unique suffering, particular to it; there are many degrees.

Do the poor souls know what is going to happen in the world?

Yes, not everything, but many things.

Do these souls tell you what is going to happen, sometimes?

They simply say that there is something in front of the door, but they don't say what. They only say what is necessary for people's conversion.

Maria, are the sufferings in Purgatory more painful than the most painful sufferings on earth?

Yes, but in a symbolic way. It hurts more in the soul.

Yes, I guess it's very difficult to describe... Does Jesus himself come to Purgatory?

No soul has ever told me so. It is the Mother of God who comes. Once I asked a poor soul if she could go to look for a soul I had been asked to find out about. She replied: "No, it is the Mother of Mercy who tells us about it."

Also, the souls in Heaven do not come to Purgatory. On the other hand, the angels are there: Saint Michael... and each soul has its guardian angel with it.

Fantastic! The angels are with us... But what do the angels do in Purgatory?

They relieve suffering and provide comfort. The souls can even see them.

Amazing! If this goes on, Maria, you're almost going to make me want to go to Purgatory, with all these stories of angels! Another question: you know, many people today believe in reincarnation. What do the souls tell you concerning this subject?

The souls say that God gives only one life.

But some would say that just one life is not enough to know God, and to have the time to be really converted, that it isn't fair. What would you reply to them?

All people have an interior faith (conscience); even if they do not practice, they recognize God implicitly. Someone who does not believe — that doesn't exist! Each soul has a conscience to recognize good and evil, a conscience given by God, an inner knowledge — in different degrees, of course, but each one knows how to discern good from evil. With this conscience, each soul can become blessed.

What happens to people who have committed suicide? Have you ever been visited by these people?

Up to now, I have never encountered the case of a suicide who was lost — this doesn't mean, of course, that that doesn't exist — but often, the souls tell me that the most guilty were those around them, when they were negligent or spread calumny.

At this moment, I asked Maria if the souls regretted having committed suicide. She answered yes. Often, suicide is due to illness.

These souls do regret their act because, as they see things in the light of God, they understand instantly all the graces that were in store for them during the time remaining for them to live — and they do see this time which remained for them, sometimes months or years — and they also see all the souls they could have helped by offering the rest of their lives to God. In the end, what hurts them most is to see the good that they could have done but didn't, because they shortened their lives. But when the cause is illness, the Lord takes this into account, of course.

Maria, have you been visited by souls who "self-destructed," by drugs, overdosing, for example?

Yes, they are not lost. It all depends on the cause of their drug-taking; but they must suffer in Purgatory.

If I tell you, for example, that I suffer too much in my body, in my heart, that it's too hard for me and I wish to die, what can I do?

Yes, this is very frequent. I would say: "My God, I can offer this suffering to save souls"; this gives renewed faith and courage. But no one says this anymore nowadays. We can also say that in doing this, the soul gains a great beatitude, a great happiness for Heaven. In Heaven, there are thousands of different types of happiness, but each one is a complete happiness; all desires are fulfilled. Each one knows he has deserved no more.

Maria, I'd like to ask you: have people from other religions — for example, Jews — come to visit you?

Yes, they are happy. Anyone who lives his faith well is happy. But it is through the Catholic faith that we gain the most for Heaven.

Are there religions which are bad for the soul?

No, but there are so many religions on earth! The closest are the Orthodox and Protestants; there are many Protestants who say the rosary; but the sects are very, very evil. Everything must be done to bring people out of them.

Are there priests in Purgatory?

(I see Maria raising her eyes to Heaven as if to say: Alas!)

Yes, there are many. They didn't promote respect for the Eucharist. So faith overall suffers. They are often in Purgatory for having neglected prayer — which has diminished their faith. But there are also many who have gone straight to Heaven!

What would you say, then, to a priest who really wants to live according to the Heart of God?

I would advise him to pray much to the Holy Spirit — and to say his rosary every day.

Maria, are there any children in Purgatory?

Yes, but Purgatory for them is not very long or painful, since they lack much discernment.

*I believe certain children have come to visit you; you were
telling me the story of this little child, the youngest one
you saw, a little girl of four. But tell me: why was she in
Purgatory?*

*Because she had received from her parents, as a Christ-
mas present, a doll. She had a twin sister who had also
received a doll.*

*This little four-year-old girl had broken her doll; se-
cretly, knowing that no one was watching her, she went to
put the broken doll in the place of her sister's, swapping
them, knowing full well in her little heart that she was going to upset her sister — and she knew very well too that it
was a lie and an injustice. Because of this, the poor girl
had to do Purgatory.*

*In fact, children often have a more tender conscience
than that of adults. It is necessary above all with them to
combat lying. They are very sensitive to untruth.*

*Maria, how can parents help to form the conscience of
their children?*

*Firstly through good example — this is the most im-
portant. Then through prayer. Parents must bless their children and instruct them well in the things of God.*

*Very important! Have you been visited by souls who, on
earth, practiced perversions? I am thinking, for example,
about the sexual domain.*

*Yes, they are not lost, but they have much to suffer to
be purified. For example, homosexuality, this truly comes
from the Evil One.*

What advice would you give, then, to all those people af-flicted by homosexuality, with this tendency in them?

Pray a lot for the strength to turn away from it. They should above all pray to the Archangel Michael; he is the great fighter par excellence against the Evil One.

What are the attitudes of heart which can lead us to losing our soul for good, I mean going to Hell?

It is when the soul does not want to go towards God, when it actually says: "I do not want."

Thank you, Maria, for making this clear.

Here I would like to mention that on this subject I questioned Vicka, one of the visionaries in Medjugorje, who also told me that those who go to Hell — and she has seen Hell — are solely those who decide to go there. It isn't God who puts someone in Hell — on the contrary, He is the Savior, He begs the soul to welcome His mercy. The sin against the Holy Spirit that Jesus speaks of, which cannot be forgiven, is the absolute refusal of mercy, and this in full awareness, full conscience. John Paul II explains this very well in his encyclical on mercy. Here too, we can do so much with prayer for souls in danger of being lost.

Maria, would you happen to have a story illustrating this?

One day, I was on a train and in my compartment there was a man who didn't stop speaking evil of the Church, of priests, even of God. I said to him: "Listen, you don't have the right to say all that, it's not good." He was furious at me. Afterwards, I arrived at my station, I got down from the train, and said to God: "Lord, do not let this soul be lost."

Years later, the soul of this man came to visit me; he told me that he had come very close to Hell, but he was saved simply by this prayer I had said at that moment!

Yes, it's extraordinary to see that just one thought, one impulse of the heart, a simple prayer for someone can prevent them from falling into Hell. It is pride which leads to Hell. Hell is to stubbornly say "NO" against God. Our prayers can elicite an act of humility in the dying, a single instant of humility, however small, which can help them to avoid Hell.

But Maria, it is incredible, all the same! How can one actually say "NO" to God at the moment of death, when one sees him?

For example, a man once told me that he did not want to go to Heaven. Why? Because God accepts injustice. I said to him that it was men, not God... He said: "I hope that I do not meet God after my death, or I will kill him with an axe."

He had a deep hatred of God. God grants man free will; he wishes each one to have his free choice.

God gives to everyone during his earthly life, and at the hour of his death, sufficient grace for conversion, even after a life spent in darkness. If one asks for forgiveness, sincerely, of course one can be saved.

Jesus said that it was difficult for a rich person to enter into the Kingdom of Heaven. Have you seen such cases?

Yes! But if they do good works, works of charity, if they practice love, they can get there, just like the poor.

Maria, do you still have visits these days from souls in Purgatory?

Yes, two or three times a week.

Really! What do you think of the practices of spiritism, for example, calling up the spirits of the departed, Ouija-boards, etc.?

It is not good. It is always evil. It is the devil who makes the table move.

It is so important to say this again and again! People really need to hear this because, nowadays, more than ever, these absurd practices are increasing dangerously!

What is the difference between what you are living with the souls of the departed, and the practices of spiritism?

We are not supposed to summon up the souls — I don't try to get them to come. In spiritism people try to call them forth.

This distinction is quite clear, and we must take it very seriously. If people were only to believe one thing I have said, I would like it to be this: those who engage in spirit-ism (moving tables, and other practices of that kind) think that they are summoning up the souls of the dead. In real-ity, if there is some response to their call, it is always and without exception Satan and his angels who are answer-

ing. People who practice spiritism (diviners, witches, etc.) are doing something very dangerous for themselves and for those who come to them for advice. They are up to their necks in lies. It is forbidden, strictly forbidden, to call up the dead. As for me, I have never done so, I do not do so, and I never will do so. When something appears to me, God alone permits it.

Of course, Satan can imitate everything that comes from God, and he does. He can imitate the voice and the appearance of the dead, but every manifestation of any kind always comes from the Evil One. Do not forget that Satan can even heal, but such healings never last.

Have you personally ever been tricked by false apparitions? For example, by the devil disguising himself as a soul in Purgatory to speak to you?

Yes. Once a soul came to see me and said to me: "Do not accept the soul which is going to come after me, because it is going to ask you for too much suffering, which you will not be able to bear; you cannot do what it is going to ask."

So, I was troubled because I remembered what my parish priest had said to me, that I had to accept each soul with generosity, and I was really troubled about whether or not to obey. So I said to myself: "Maybe it's the demon who is before me and not a soul in Purgatory; the demon in disguise?" I said to this soul: "If you are the demon, go away!"

At once he gave out a loud scream and left. In fact, the soul who came after him was a soul who had real need of my help; it was very important for me to listen to this soul!

When the devil appears, does holy water always make him leave?

It disturbs him very much and he flees at once.

Maria, you are now very well known, especially in Germany and Austria, but also throughout Europe, thanks to your talk and your book. At the beginning, however, you were very hidden. How did it happen that, overnight, people recognized that your supernatural experience was authentic?

It was when the souls asked me to tell their families to give back goods which had been acquired dishonestly. They saw that what I said was true.

At this point, Maria related several testimonies, too long to quote here. Several times souls came to find her, saying: "Go to my family in such and such a village" — which Maria did not know — "and tell my father, my son, my brother to give back a certain property or amount of money which I acquired dishonestly. I will be delivered from Purgatory when these goods are given back." Maria would have all the details of the field, or exact amount of money, or the property concerned, and the family would be staggered to discover that she knew all these details, because sometimes even they didn't know that these goods had been acquired dishonestly by their relative. Through this, Maria began to be very well-known.

Maria, is there official recognition by the Church of this particular charism that you practice with regard to the souls in Purgatory, and also with regard to those who are touched by your apostolate?

My bishop told me that as long as there are no theological errors, I should continue: he has okay'd it. My parish priest, who is also my spiritual guide, confirms these things too.

I would like to ask you a question that may be indiscreet: you have done so much for the poor souls that surely, when you die, in your turn, thousands of souls will be your escort into Heaven; I think that you certainly won't have to pass through Purgatory!

I don't believe I will go straight to Heaven without time in Purgatory because I have had more light, more knowledge, and therefore my faults are more serious. But all the same, I hope that the souls will help me rise to Heaven!

Certainly! And Maria, do you enjoy this charism? Or is it something burdensome and difficult for you, all these requests from souls?

No, I do not pay much attention to the difficulty, for I know I can help them so much. I can help many souls and I am very happy to do this.

Maria, I would like to thank you also in the name of all readers for this beautiful testimony. But please permit me one last question: so that we might know you better, would you be so good as to tell us a few words about your life?

Well... from when I was little I wanted to enter a convent, but Mother told me to wait until I was twenty. I did not wish to get married. Mother had told me a good deal about the souls in Purgatory and, already at school, these souls helped me a lot. So I said to myself that I had to do everything for them.

After school, I thought about entering a convent; I entered the Sisters of the Heart of Jesus, but they told me that my health was too poor to stay with them. As a child, I had had pneumonia and pleurisy. The Superior had confirmed my religious vocation but advised me to enter an easier order, to wait for some years. I wanted above all a cloistered order, and right away!

But after two more attempts, the conclusion was the same: my health was too poor. So I said to myself that entering a convent wasn't God's will for me. I suffered mentally a great deal. I said to myself that the Lord had not shown me what he wanted of me.

Up to the moment he entrusted me with this task for the souls in Purgatory, at the age of twenty-five, he'd made me wait eight years.

At home, there were eight of us children. I worked on our farm, starting at the age of fifteen; then I went to Germany as a servant for a peasant family. Afterwards, I worked here at the farm in Sonntag.

From the age of twenty-five, when the souls began to come, I had much to suffer for them — Now I am much better physically. So, there you are...

It was indeed a real pleasure for me to meet Maria Simma, a woman whose life is one of complete devotion. Each second, each hour of her life has a weight of eternity, not only for herself but for so many souls, known or unknown, that she, in many different ways and with so much love, has helped deliver from Purgatory and enjoy the eternal happiness of Heaven.

Tommaso Pollaci - *Messa in Suffragio delle Anime Purganti*
(Mass for the Intention of the Souls in Purgatory)

-3-

A Proposition to All

Now, I have a proposition to make to each one of you: we could make the decision that none of us will go to Purgatory!

This is really possible, we have everything in our hands to make it come true. I remember the words of St. John of the Cross: he says that the Providence of God always provides, in every life, the purification that is needed to allow us to go straight to Heaven at the hour of death.

Providence puts enough difficulties in our lives, trials, suffering, sickness, hardships — so that all these purifications, if we accept them, may be enough to bring us straight to Heaven.

Why doesn't this happen? Because we rebel, we do not welcome with love, with gratitude, these gifts of trials in our lives, and we sin by rebelling, by non-submission if you prefer.

So, let us ask the Lord for the grace to seize every opportunity so that on the day of our death he sees us shining with purity and beauty.

Of course, if we decide on this, I do not say that the way will be easy, since — let's remember this — the Lord never promised that the way would be easy but our way will be in peace, and it will be a path of happiness: the Lord will be with us. Above all — and this is what I would like to stress here — let us make the most of the time which remains to us on earth, this time which is so precious, during which we are still given the chance to grow in love. This means to grow towards the Glory to come and the beauty which is destined for us. Each minute, we can still grow in love, but the souls in Purgatory can no longer grow.

Even the angels envy us this power we have to grow each minute in love while we are on earth.

Each little act of love we offer to the Lord, each little sacrifice or fast, each little privation or battle against our tendencies, our faults, each little forgiveness of our enemy, all the things we can offer of this sort, will be later for us an ornament, a jewel, a real treasure for eternity.

So, let us seize every opportunity to be as beautiful as God desires us to be already in his prescience. If we saw in its full light the splendor of a pure soul, of a soul purified, then we would cry for joy and wonder, because of its beauty!

A human soul is something of great splendor before God; this is why God desires us to be perfectly pure. It is not by being faultless in our ways that we will become pure. No, it is through our repentance of our sins, and our humility. You see, it's quite different! The saints are not "faultless" souls, but those who get up again and again each time they fall, and ask forgiveness; it's very different. So, let us make use of the wonderful means the Lord puts into our hands to help the souls still waiting to possess God and who yearn because of this delay, because of this splendid God they have already perceived and whom they desire with all their hearts.

Also, we mustn't forget that the prayer of children has an immense power over the heart of God. So, let's teach our children to pray. I remember a little girl to whom I had spoken about the poor souls. I said to her: "Now, you're going to pray for the souls of all the members of your family and friends who are already dead. Would you like to go before Jesus and ask him?"

She went before Jesus, and five minutes later she returned, and I asked her: "What did you ask the Lord?"

She answered: " I asked the Lord to deliver all the souls in Purgatory!"

This answer struck me greatly and I realized I'd been miserly in my request, but she had understood straight away what to ask for. Children sense so much, they can obtain so much from the heart of God.

Also, let's mention here retired people and all those who have free time; if they went to Mass often, daily... What a treasure of grace they would store up, not only for themselves but for their deceased and for thousands of souls!

The value of one single Mass is immeasurable. If we only realized!...

What riches our ignorance, our indifference, or simply our laziness lead us to waste!

Whereas we have the power in our hands to save our brothers, by becoming co-redeemers ourselves, together with Jesus our Savior and our Redeemer!

Fra. Angelico - *Cristo al Limbo*
(Chist's Decent into Limbo)

-4-

Don't Forget About Indulgences!

M other Church has some wonderful treasures in store
for us — let's take a closer look at some of them!

*"Through indulgences the faithful can obtain the re-
mission of temporal punishment resulting from sins
for themselves and also for the souls of Purgatory"*
(Catechism of the Catholic Church, §1498)

What is an indulgence? Here is what the *Catechism of
the Catholic Church* has to say:

*"An indulgence is a remission before God of the tem-
poral punishment due to sins whose guilt has already
been forgiven, which the faithful Christian who is
duly disposed gains under certain prescribed conditions through the action of the Church which, as the
minister of redemption, dispenses and applies with*

authority the treasury of the satisfactions of Christ and the saints.

"An indulgence is partial or plenary according as it removes either part or all of the temporal punishment due to sin." Indulgences may be applied to the living or the dead." (§1471)

Jesus gave to his disciples, and therefore to the Church, the power to bind and to loose, and down through the centuries, in many different ways, the Church has used this channel of the mercy of God towards the living and the dead.

Everything concerning indulgences was revised by Pope Paul VI; the results can be found in *The Book of Indulgences*, Rules and Grants, published June 29, 1968 (Vatican Publishers).

"The aim pursued by ecclesiastical authority in granting indulgences is not only that of helping the faithful to expiate the punishment due to sin, but also that of urging them to perform works of piety, penitence and charity—particularly those which lead to growth in faith and which favor the common good."

"And if the faithful offer indulgences in suffrage for the dead, they cultivate charity in an excellent way and while raising their minds to heaven they bring a wiser order into the things of this world."

"Although indulgences are in fact free gifts, nevertheless they are granted for the living as well as for the dead only on determined conditions...the faithful have to love God, detest sin, place their trust in the merits of Christ and believe firmly in the great assistance they derive from the communion of saints."

As a result of the reform, all distinctions of day, month, and year have been abolished; the only distinction retained is that between *plenary* and *partial indulgence*.

We should also note the following:

- No one can give the indulgence he obtains to another person who is still living.
- Both plenary and partial indulgences can always be given for the dead.

"The faithful who use with devotion an object of piety (crucifix, cross, rosary, scapular or medal) properly blessed by any priest, can acquire a partial indulgence. But if this object is blessed by the Supreme Pontiff or any bishop, the faithful who use it devoutly can also acquire a plenary indulgence on the feast of the Holy Apostles Peter and Paul, provided they also make a profession of faith using any legitimate formula."

THE AMAZING SECRET OF THE SOULS IN PURGATORY

In Medjugorje, on July 18, 1995, Our Lady said:

"Dear children, today I call you to place more blessed objects in your homes and call everyone to put some blessed object on their person. Bless all objects, and thus Satan will attack you less because you will have armor against him."

"To acquire a plenary undulgence it is necessary to perform the work to which the indulgence is attached and to fulfill three conditions: sacramental confession, Eucharistic Communion and prayer for the intentions of the Supreme Pontiff. It is further required that all attachment to sin, even to venial sin, be absent."

The condition of praying for the Supreme Pontiff's intention is fully satisfied by reciting one "Our Father" and one "Hail Mary." Nevertheless, the individual faithful are free to recite any other prayer according to their own piety and devotion toward the Supreme Pontiff.

The new reform provides for three concessions:

1. **Partial indulgence is granted to the faithful who, in fulfilling their duties and in facing the adversities of life, raise their soul to God with humble confidence, and add in their heart a pious invocation.**

2. **Partial indulgence is granted to the faithful who, with a soul full of faith and mercy, give themselves or their goods to their brothers in need.**

3. **Partial indulgence is granted to the faithful who, in a spirit of repentance, deprive themselves spontaneously of something.**

Plenary indulgence can be obtained on the following occasions:

- adoration of the Blessed Sacrament for at least one half-hour;
- recitation of the entire rosary in church, as a family or in community;
- making the Stations of the Cross;
- reading Holy Scripture for at least one half-hour;
- a church visit between noon of November 1 and midnight of November 2, for the intention of the deceased;
- visiting a cemetery, for the intention of the deceased;
- taking part in a First Holy Communion ceremony, or the first Mass of a priest, or the anniversary of 25, 50, or 60 years of priesthood;
- renewing one's baptismal promises during the Easter Vigil;
- adoration of the Cross during the Good Friday liturgy;
- papal benediction, even when received listening to the radio or watching on television.

By going to confession regularly, one can obtain many plenary indulgences.

Only one plenary indulgence a day is permitted, but one may obtain a number of partial indulgences on one day by reciting certain prayers suggested by the Church, such as:

- To you, Blessed Joseph
- *Angelus Domini*
- Soul of Christ, sanctify me
- Act of Spiritual Communion
- The Creed
- The Office of the Dead
- Psalm 130 *(De profundis)*
- Litanies of the Most Holy Name of Jesus
- Litanies of the Sacred Heart of Jesus
- Litanies of the Most Precious Blood
- Litanies of the Blessed Virgin Mary
- Litanies of Saint Joseph
- Litanies of the Saints
- *Magnificat*
- Remember, O most gracious Virgin Mary
- Psalm 51 *(Miserere)*
- Prayer for priestly or religious vocations
- Prayer for Unity of the Christians
- *Salve Regina* (Hail, Holy Queen)
- Sign of the Cross (devoutly done)
- *Tantum ergo* (Let us adore the Sacrament)
- *Te Deum*
- *Veni Creator* (Come, Holy Spirit)

This list is not complete.

Partial indulgences are obtained through concrete acts of faith, hope, and love, in the midst of the trials of life and as we carry out the duties of our daily lives. Indulgences are also obtained by acts of charity towards our neighbor, voluntary fasting, and ejaculatory prayers or spontaneous thoughts addressed to God, to the Blessed Mother, to the Holy Family. *The Book of Indulgences* contains a list of suggested prayers; it is a precious book — read it!

Yes, Divine Heart of Jesus,

Grant me the grace always to live according to your will, as much in the finest, most joyful, most important moments of my life as in the difficult moments.

Grant me always to be ready for my last hour; give me the courage to give everything for your love, even my life, if necessary.

Jesus, through your most Holy and painful Passion, may your coming at the hour of my death find me awake, like a good servant, with true repentance, a good confession, fortified by the last sacraments.

Lord, do not abandon me in my last struggle on this earth, when I will have to battle against Satan, perhaps raging in fury. May your Holy Mother, the Mother of Mercy, and Saint Michael and all the angels, help and protect me against all temptation at the hour I leave this world. May they strengthen and console me in my pain.

Grant me, Lord, at that hour, a living faith, a firm trust, an ardent love and a great patience.

Help me to commit myself fully, in all clarity of mind, into your hands and to abandon myself like a little child to your holy peace.

In your infinite goodness and your great mercy, O Jesus, remember me! Amen.